Franklin's Daughters

Distributed by
University of Pennsylvania Press
Philadelphia, Pennsylvania 19104-4011

ISBN 0-8122-1813-2

Text design by Creative Communications, University of Pennsylvania

Franklin's Daughters

Profiles of Penn Women

Linda Mallon
and Anita Sama

125 YEARS

WOMEN at PENN

Acknowledgements

The authors owe a debt of gratitude to many who, for months, have searched their personal files and those of their institutions to bring together, in some cases for the first time, information on 22 remarkable women.

Thanks especially to these individuals at Penn: Jeff Cromarty, James M. Duffin, Bonnie Eisner, Martin Hackett, Nicholas G. Heavens, Ryan Janda, Mark Frazier Lloyd, Joan Lynaugh, John Shea And elsewhere: Susan Abrams, *Bulletin of the History of Medicine;* Lucienne Beard, Alice Paul Centennial Foundation; Jim Bohning, Department of Chemistry, Lehigh University; Joan Di Martino, Kentucky Historical Society; Sister Elizabeth Ann Eckhart, Sisters of Saint John the Divine; Donald Glassman, Barnard College; Lee Grady, McCormick-International Harvester Collection, State Historical Society of Wisconsin; Joanne Grossman, Archives, Medical College of Pennsylvania – Hahnemann University; Dorothy Kapenstein, Alumnae Association, The Philadelphia High School for Girls; Lea Kemp, Rochester Museum and Science Center; Geraldine Myles, The Philadelphia High School for Girls; Dr. Steven Peitzman, Medical College of Pennsylvania – Hahnemann University; Professor Rosalind Rosenberg, Barnard College; Brian Rutzen, ATO Archives, University of Illinois at Champaign-Urbana; Professor Rudolf Schmid, Department of Integrative Biology, University of California, Berkeley; Wilma Slaight, Wellesley College Library; Donna Wells, Howard University Library. We are grateful for the willing and resourceful research accomplished by Christian Mueller, Lucy Mueller, Janis Roihl, and Emily Sama Martin.

Thanks also are owed to fellow Penn alumnae who gave their time to help shepherd this work to completion: Loretta Barrett, Judy Berkowitz, and Caryn Karmatz-Rudy.

And to our families, who were patient for months as our files and this project took over our homes and our time.

Clearly, credit for the collection of this material belongs to many. Responsibility for any errors in its synthesis is entirely our own.

Linda Mallon
Anita Sama

Preface

The year 2001 marks the 125th anniversary of women at the University of Pennsylvania. When we started planning this celebration two years ago, we could little imagine where it would lead, and could scarcely have expected either the overwhelming gratitude it has engendered or the discoveries it has provoked. First and foremost among the discoveries has been the women themselves, the pioneers who overcame enormous obstacles to pave the way not only for their own incredible successes but for our opportunities and privileges as well.

Singly, these women stand out on their own for their brilliance, tenacity, and extraordinary contributions to Penn and to society at large. Together, whether they knew it or not, they pried open the doors of higher education and made possible a modern coeducational experience that Penn women and men now take for granted. Women certainly owe much to the women's rights movement; yet one cannot and should not underestimate the importance of those women, driven less by politics than by an unyielding will to learn and to advance, who paved the way for the Penn women of today.

This book is dedicated to those brave women, as well as the dreams that carried them forward. It is inspired by their strength and persistence as much as by their incredible accomplishments. Where some women in the past saw barriers, the women profiled in the book vaulted over the many hurdles set in their way and found opportunity. Let us not forget what they had to overcome, but let us be inspired by the stories of their ingenuity and fortitude, by their untiring dedication to others, and mostly by their will to pursue their dreams.

My heartfelt thanks to the many Penn women who made this book possible. First to Loretta Barrett, who immediately understood its importance and guided us through the whole process, and to Caryn Karmatz-Rudy, whose help was invaluable. Next, to our writers, Linda Mallon and Anita Sama, who delivered everything they promised and more despite many time pressures. Also, a note of gratitude to our distinguished faculty committee led by Professor Rebecca Bushnell and Dr. Barbara Lowery, associate provost, for their hours of e-mails and guidance. A special thank-you is due to Mark Frazier Lloyd, the University's archivist, for his devotion to the success of the whole celebration and without whom we could not have chronicled our history so carefully.

This books stops in the sixties when women became more numerous but Penn was still one of the few elite Ivy League institutions to offer its degree equally to women. I am sure the sequel, *Franklin's Daughters, Volume 2,* will be equally inspiring.

Judith Roth Berkowitz
Chair
125th Celebration

Table of Contents

Introduction

Writing in 1749, Benjamin Franklin called for the creation of an institution in Philadelphia whose academic environment would be devoted to practical application for the greater good:

"The whole should be constantly inculcated and cultivated, that Benignity of Mind, which shows itself in searching for and seizing every Opportunity to serve and to oblige."

That institution became the University of Pennsylvania. And while Franklin may not have anticipated it, since they first stepped onto campus the women of Penn have taken his concept of enlightened service and made it their own.

This became abundantly clear to us when we embarked on our mission to mark 125 years of women at Penn. As students, faculty, administrators, and trustees; in science, medicine, law, and education; in service to the University and to the wider world; the dedication of Penn's women to useful purpose is a recurrent theme.

Penn men surely share this heritage. But we were reminded of the adage about Ginger Rogers — that she did everything Fred Astaire did, but backwards and in heels. Over and over again, the women of Penn used their education to improve the lives of others. And against such odds!

Many chose marriage over career as the only way to continue the latter. Others managed to combine the two, and to even slip in motherhood. They all battled sexism — and some battled racism — in the classroom and at work. And yet they loved what they did. Bitterness rarely breaks through in the tattered notes, letters, and documents that for some are their only written legacy.

More often expressed were lively intelligence, graciousness, and, best of all, a sense of humor that shielded them from the crushing disapproval of a society not yet ready to accept them as scholars and leaders first, mothers and wives second.

Promise and Progress

While girls were part of Franklin's early affiliated Charity School, society at the time dictated their exclusion from the college-preparatory Academy of Philadelphia and the college that followed it. The University grew, gaining a charter from the young government of Pennsylvania, adding schools of law, medicine, and a predecessor to the School of Engineering. None admitted women.

When the trustees closed the Charity School, leaving instruction of poor children to the city of Philadelphia, the educational trust fund was redirected to collegiate scholarships for young men and to instruction for poor "female students" if authorized by the Provost. Other young women who wanted to attend lectures in

1

history and courses in chemistry and physics could do so for a fee. But unlike men, they would receive no degree.

The Trustees Resolved:

"Any female attending said course of instruction may present herself at the end thereof for examination therein and if said examination is satisfactory shall receive from the authorities of the University a certificate thereof."

It was under this arrangement that two young women quietly enrolled as special students in the department of chemistry on October 13, 1876.

Slowly, sometimes painfully, other avenues within the University opened. By 1879, "persons of both sexes are now admitted" to undergraduate instruction in English, classics, history, social science, speculative philosophy, music, general chemistry, physics, and analytical chemistry. In some instances, they were welcomed; in others, merely tolerated.

As the progressive ideas of the 19th century gained acceptance in the Western world, higher education for women gained ground in America and at Penn.

In 1882, the Graduate School of Arts and Sciences was founded, becoming the first school to admit women from its inception to courses leading to a degree. There was even a movement by some faculty and trustees to establish a "women's section" in the undergraduate college. The proposal was defeated, but the trustees agreed to allow a college for women at Penn "so soon as funds are received sufficient to meet the expense thereof." More than 40 years would pass before this promise was fulfilled.

By the 1920s, 17 different academic programs admitted women. Some women attended part time, but nearly 2,000 were aiming for degrees. Over half of those were in the School of Education. A quarter were pursuing master's degrees and doctorates in a variety of fields. With no housing provided, many found lodging off campus or commuted from home. To begin to accommodate them, the University purchased an apartment building at 34 and Walnut and converted it to Sergeant Hall — the first women's dormitory and soon the lively center of numerous women's student organizations, including a separate student government and newspaper. Bennett Hall opened in 1925 and functioned as the academic heart of women's education for 40 years. The long-awaited College of Liberal Arts for Women conferred its first degrees in 1934.

By the 1950s, the numbers of women on campus had increased dramatically to more than 4,000. There were now women on the faculty and sitting on the University's board of trustees. In 1960 Hill Hall, the first building expressly constructed for women students, opened its doors, allowing more women to live on campus. Women were becoming an essential part of the Penn community. Men's and women's activities merged, and in 1968, Hey Day, which had been separated by gender for 40 years, became a joint celebration.

A Heritage Restored

Early in Benjamin Franklin's autobiography, he recounts the story of his correspondence with a young friend:

"A question was once somehow or other started between Collins and me on the propriety of educating the female sex in learning and their abilities for study. He was of the opinion that it was improper and that they were naturally unequal to it. I took the contrary side...."

At the time, society sided with the now-forgotten Collins.

But in 2001, Penn has proven Franklin's early instinct correct. Women and men work together to carry forward the University's long tradition of scholarship coupled with service to society. What was once a trickle of women scholars has become a flood.

This anniversary volume depicts some of the struggles and successes of Penn's female pioneers. Space and time limited the number, but it's important that these stories be told. Immersed in the egalitarian Penn of today, female students might take their advantages for granted. They are actively creating their own history, but they are also continuing a valuable collective tradition —Franklin's daughters all.

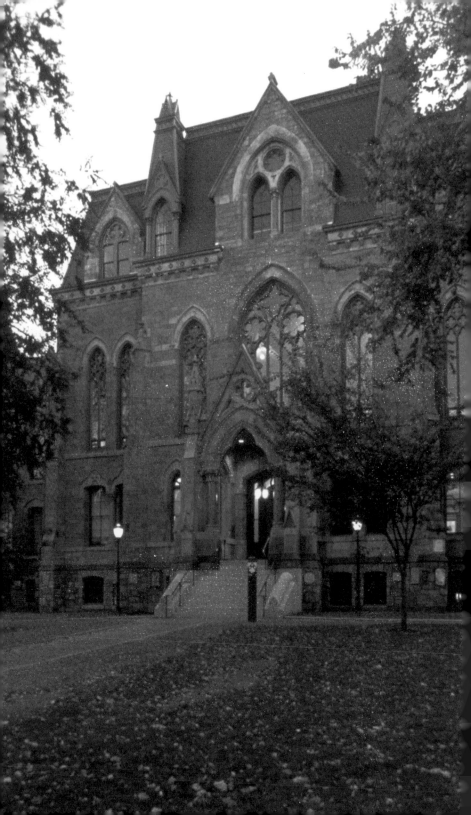

Profiles

Easby, Flanigen, Gannett

The picture shows three young women in bustles and long aprons, their hair neatly coiffed, their demeanor serious. Unlikely revolutionaries. But make no mistake, Gertrude Peirce Easby, Anna Lockhart Flanigen, and Mary Lewis Gannett had a radical agenda: They wanted to attend classes at the University of Pennsylvania, a shocking prospect in 1876.

We are all beneficiaries of their determination.

Flanigen and Easby were science students at Philadelphia's Women's Medical College when they first approached Frederick Genth, chair of Penn's chemistry department, with a request that they be allowed to take courses.

Initially, they were rebuffed. But Genth was sympathetic to their cause, and when the emperor and empress of Brazil toured the Penn campus as part of Philadelphia's Centennial Exhibition, Genth took advantage of the bonhomie of the moment and put Easby and Flanigen's request directly to the assembled board of trustees. It was granted.

Joined in their studies by Gannett, Flanigen and Easby were quiet in victory. They had to be. "We used to work for seven or eight hours a day in the laboratory," Easby remembered in a 1941 newspaper interview. "During that time we never said a word to any of the boys working side by side with us and they never said a word to us. You see, it was outrageous enough in the first place that we should be allowed to attend a man's class. But to talk to any of the students — well, that wouldn't have done at all."

Silent, but not inactive. To show their Penn spirit, the women sewed red and blue ribbons onto their laboratory aprons. And while ignored in class, they made friends on campus. Easby recalled regularly walking to class with one of the male students. Upon reaching the laboratory building, they split up and entered separately.

In 1878, after two years of study, Flanigen and Easby were awarded certificates of proficiency, an acknowledgement of their expertise, rather than an official degree. Gannett continued her studies for another year. And then they went their separate ways.

Flanigen was the only one to pursue a career in chemistry. After receiving her certificate, she took up post-graduate research under the direction of Dr. Edgar Fahs Smith, a mentor to many of Penn's first women students. When he left Penn to take up a short-term position at Muhlenberg College, she found work as a chemist and assayer at the Keystone Watch Case Company of Philadelphia. Flanigen would work there for 15 years before finally going abroad to study in London and Berlin.

Mary Gannett

She returned to take a faculty position at Mount Holyoke College and to pursue a Penn doctorate in chemistry. In 1905 at the age of 54, Flanigen received her degree. She continued to teach at Mount Holyoke College, rising to the rank of assistant professor in the chemistry department before retiring.

Gannett left science behind but spent the rest of her life advocating women's rights. She married, Rev. William C. Gannett, a Unitarian minister, in 1887. Moving to Rochester, N.Y,. in 1889, the two became a formidable force in that city's progressive reform movements. Among other accomplishments, the

Gannetts in 1889 helped found the Boys Evening Home, which offered classes, accommodations, and support to under-privileged boys. In 1893, Gannett and Susan B. Anthony joined forces to create the Women's Educational and Industrial Union, which provided legal aid for poor women and kindergarten classes for their children.

Under the auspices of the Women's Ethical Club, which she founded, Gannett successfully battled to open the University of Rochester to women and, later, to African-Americans. And as an ardent suf-fragette, Gannett frequently spoke out against the assertion that women did not want the vote. "Try to persuade any man that he will have more weight, more influ-ence, if he gives up his vote, allies himself with no party, and relies on influence to achieve his ends!" she said in a speech at the National American Woman Suffrage Association's convention in 1908. "By all

Gertrude Easby

means let us use to its utmost whatever influence we have, but in all justice do not ask us to be content with this."

After receiving her certificate, Easby continued her studies at Penn in a postgraduate course and was a co-author, with Dr. Smith, of a paper on the products obtained in the nitration of meta chlorsalicylic acid. In 1884 she married Francis Easby, a Penn engineering graduate, and gave up her career to follow his. "I never made practical use of my chemistry," she wrote many years later, "but the work had a distinct influence on my life."

So did her experience as one of Penn's first co-eds. "I want to urge women to go in for original work in research — no longer to be merely hands for another brain," she wrote in 1929. "I want to see women produce work which is the result of their own clear and independent thought."

Active in women's volunteer organizations, she served a term as secretary of the Association for the Advancement of Women and was one of the first women to serve as director of Baltimore's Female House of Refuge, which was set up to care for delinquent girls and train them for re-entry into society. Easby never relinquished her attachment to the University and marched in the alumni parade at Penn's bicentennial in 1940. At that occasion she remarked, not a little indignantly, "If we had had a parade when I went to college, I feel sure that, in spite of the fact that women at Penn were regarded as freaks, I would have marched right up with my own class."

Alice Bennett

Who says there are no second acts in American lives?

Consider Alice Bennett. One of the pioneering women physicians in America, Bennett gained early prominence for her innovative treatment of mental illness in women, only to be sidelined by controversy in middle age. Yet, by the time of her death in New York at the age of 74, Bennett was celebrated for her devotion to maternity care in the slums of New York. Bennett's beginnings were humble. She was born in Wrentham, Mass., the second daughter and youngest of six children of Isaac Francis Bennett, a blacksmith, and Lydia Hayden. As a young woman, she taught for four years in the Wrentham district schools in order to pay for her college education.

In 1872, Bennett entered the Women's Medical College in Philadelphia. She graduated with a medical degree in 1876, and in 1880 she became the first woman to receive a Ph.D. from the University of Pennsylvania, having studied anatomy at the Auxiliary School of Medicine. This degree program was later discontinued and the auxiliary school closed, but a modern corollary is the Biomedical Graduate Studies Program, which awards degrees through the School of Arts and Sciences.

The same year that she graduated from Penn, Bennett was appointed superintendent of the Department for Women at the Norristown Hospital for the Insane. The first woman to hold that position, she was

Born: 1851 Died: 1925

in the vanguard of a movement that advocated using female physicians in the treatment of mentally ill women.

Bennett served at Norristown for 16 years. Beginning with one patient and one nurse, the program expanded under Bennett's tenure to 1,027 female patients, two assistant physicians, one pathologist, one pharmacist, and 106 nurses. Among her many accomplishments was the creation of occupational and educational therapy programs as an alternative to heavy medical sedation. Bennett was a strong opponent of the use of physical restraint, writing in 1881: "I can have no shadow of doubt that extraordinary precautions often suggest, or increase, the violence they are intended to prevent. Freedom of action is a wonderful tranquilizer." She also began the practice of regular gynecological exams for her patients and, as a result of her experience, began to refute the common belief that women's emotional and mental disorders arose from their reproductive systems.

But she became engulfed in a firestorm of controversy in 1892 when local newspapers reported that she had allowed other doctors to perform ovariectomies on her patients without their consent.

While Bennett was cleared of any wrongdoing in the matter, when she was offered a position in 1896 as attending physician to Virginia McCormick, the mentally ill daughter of industrialist Cyrus McCormick, Bennett decided to leave Norristown.

From correspondence at the time, it is clear that Bennett had learned to be vigilant in her own defense. While negotiating her salary with Cyrus McCormick, Jr., McCormick's son, Bennett suggested that the pay for her three-year contract be invested in advance to assure her of an income even if the arrangement fell through.

As it happens, it did. After two years service, moving her patient among the various McCormick family estates, Bennett was accused of morphine addiction by several of the nurses attending Virginia McCormick. Admitting that she occasionally medicated herself for menstrual difficulties, rheumatism, or hay fever, Bennett, however, strenuously denied any form of addiction. Nevertheless, she resigned her position and retreated to her hometown of Wrentham to take up private practice.

There she could have quietly ended her days. But in 1910, at the age of 59, Bennett moved to New York to join Dr. Emily Blackwell's New York Infirmary for Women and Children on Tompkins Square. She worked at the free clinic for 15 years without pay as director of maternity care, assisting women from the poorest neighborhoods of Manhattan and Brooklyn.

Although it is widely believed to be named for her, Penn's Bennett Hall is actually the legacy of Col. Joseph Bennett, who deeded to the University a group of row houses he owned at the corner of 34th and Walnut.

But Alice Bennett's legacy is formidable — it comes in the 2,000 safe deliveries over which she presided, and in the uncounted lives, both maternal and infant, that she saved through her expertise and care.

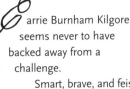

Carrie Kilgore

Born: 1838 Died: 1909

*C*arrie Burnham Kilgore seems never to have backed away from a challenge.

Smart, brave, and feisty, she argued her way into a profession that did not want her, becoming in 1883 the first woman to graduate from the University of Pennsylvania Law School. It was a battle she was, by temperament and choice, uniquely suited to fight.

Kilgore was born into prosperity: her father, James Burnham, was a successful wool manufacturer in Craftsbury, Vt., and her mother, Eliza Arnold, a schoolteacher and artist. But she was orphaned young and her guardians required her to work long hours in the family factory and kitchen. By the age of 15, she was also teaching school in an effort to earn enough money to further her own education. Felled by a bout of typhoid, Kilgore moved to Sun Prairie, Wisc., to live with an older sister. There, she spent five years preparing male seminarians at the State Normal School for college. The irony of her position did not escape her. "Young men whom I prepared in Latin, Greek, and mathematics were received into the State University one year in advance, while its doors were closed to me because I was a woman," she remarked years later.

In 1863, Kilgore entered the Hygeio-Therapeutic College of Bellevue Hospital in New York to study physiology and anatomy. She also enrolled in New York's Boston Normal Insitute for Physical Education, receiving her medical degree from that institution a year later. But medicine was not her true calling.

Having moved to Philadelphia to head the French School for Young Ladies, Kilgore began reading law under the guidance of Damon Young Kilgore, a lawyer she'd met previously in Wisconsin and whom she later married. She progressed quickly and after a year of apprenticeship sought permission in 1871 to attend law lectures at Penn.

The response was not kindly. In a letter she wrote years later to Margaret Klingelsmith, who followed in her footsteps at the law school, Kilgore recalled the reaction of the dean of the law school: "When I made application to E. Spencer Miller for the opportunity to attend his lectures and to study law in the University as a student, he replied as follows: 'I do not know what the board of trustees will do, but as for me, if they admit a woman I will resign for I will neither lecture to niggers nor women.'"

Kilgore did not back down, and a long battle was joined, not just to study law (she was finally admitted to the law school in 1881) but also to practice it. After years of unsuccessful litigation seeking admission for herself (and all women) to practice in various Philadelphia and Pennsylvania courts, Kilgore switched strategies. In an end run around the local courts that had been blocking her admission, Kilgore petitioned state legislators to create a bill guaranteeing that any lawyer admitted to practice before the state's higher courts could be admitted to practice before any court in the commonwealth. The bill passed in 1886, and within the year Kilgore was practicing before the Supreme Court of Pennsylvania (and all the lower courts feeding into it). In 1890, she was admitted to the U.S. Supreme Court.

Not surprisingly, Kilgore believed that suffrage was key to the broader acceptance of women into schools and professions of their choice. As early as 1872, Kilgore appeared as a plaintiff before the Pennsylvania Supreme Court in a test case for voting rights. She did not prevail, but her argument before the court became a rallying cry for others: "It is not simply whether I shall be protected in the exercise of my inalienable right and duty of self-government," Kilgore warned, "but whether a government, the mere agent of the people, based upon the equality of all mankind, and which 'derives its just powers from the consent of the governed,' can deny to any portion of its intelligent, adult citizens participation therein and still hold them amendable to its laws."

After the death of her husband, Kilgore assumed his private practice for a number of years, eventually serving as the first woman solicitor for a corporation. She remained combative. Writing to Klingelsmith in 1902, Kilgore chided: "It is impossible for you, or indeed any of the University people, not then connected with the University, to appreciate the intense opposition to my admission to the University, and the work required to open the way for and to women."

True to form, Kilgore never stopped seeking out challenges. Just a year before she died, Kilgore posted a final first on her résumé: She rode in the inaugural balloon ascension of the Philadelphia Aeronautical Recreation Society.

Emily Gregory

$\mathcal{E}$ mily Lovira Gregory was a brilliant botanist. But she nurtured more than just plants; she worked tirelessly at broadening educational opportunities for other women. Lecturing without pay, reaching into her own pocket to cover the salaries of laboratory assistants, and battling bureaucracies to obtain space and equipment for her students, Gregory always endeavored to smooth the path of those who were following in her footsteps.

Gregory was born in Portage, N.Y., to David and Calista Stone Gregory. As a young woman, she took up teaching in order to save enough money to go on to college. It wasn't until 1876, when she was 35, that Gregory achieved her goal and enrolled at Cornell. She graduated in 1881 with a degree in English literature and a minor in botany, but seems to have immediately put literature aside in order to concentrate on science .

Because European universities were generally more open to women students, Gregory traveled abroad for graduate work. But even there, she met resistance. In order to audit the Berlin lectures of the famed Swiss botanist Simon Schwendener, Gregory had to seat herself behind a curtain in an anteroom in back of the lecture platform. When she found errors in the published research of another botanist, Gregory approached Schwendener to point out the discrepancies. He curtly informed her that she must be wrong because women did not possess enough intelligence for scientific study. Quietly and politely (and in

Born: 1841 Died: 1897

German), Gregory argued her case. At the end of the day she had convinced Schwendener of two things: that she was right, and that at least one woman's mind was capable of scientific reasoning. Charmed, Schwendener became her mentor — and remained so for the rest of her life.

Gregory received her doctorate from the University of Zurich in 1886 yet she was unable to find employment when she returned home. In a letter written about that time she reports with some exasperation: "After fitting myself for doing advanced work in the science of botany, which I did by four years' work in college at Cornell, followed by four years' work in Universities abroad, I found to my surprise that there was little opportunity for me to teach in the grade for which I had prepared."

After a brief unpaid stint at Bryn Mawr, Gregory moved to the University of Pennsylvania. While she was doing research there, several women applied to study in the biology department. The faculty agreed to take them on if Gregory would teach them. Although she received no payment for her work, Gregory accepted the position and became Penn's first woman teaching fellow.

She moved to Barnard College in 1889, but maintained a connection to Penn, hiring several of her students as assistants in the botany laboratory she created at Barnard. Her enthusiasm for her subject, and for her students, is legendary. "She was not clear nor concise in her lectures and quizzes, but this came from her desire to impart all that she could of the wealth of information she had in store," wrote a colleague.

In what turned out to be a final exercise of scientific analysis, Gregory in late middle age chronicled her personal struggle with religious faith. Having embraced Darwin, how could she accept God? Characteristically, she recognized this as a teachable moment for others. The result was the pamphlet "A Scientist's Confession of Faith; The Short Story of a Long Journey." It was virtually the last thing she published, for within months, Gregory was dead from pneumonia.

Greatly mourned at her death, Gregory's memory is preserved at Barnard through an annual teaching award. At Penn, her mission continues in the form of Gregory College House, the modern language residential project that actively encourages mentoring relationships between students and faculty.

Ida Asbury

Born: 1870 Died: 1955

Ida Bowser Asbury was born shortly after the Civil War into the comparative comfort of Philadelphia's African-American middle class. Little is known about her early life. And yet when Asbury stood with the University of Pennsylvania Class of 1890 at the Philadelphia Academy of Music to receive a certificate of proficiency in music, she carried the double distinction of being the first African-American woman to graduate from the music department and the first to enroll at Penn.

Asbury came from an artistic family. Her father, David Bowser, was an ornamental painter and her mother, Elizabeth Grey, a regalia maker. For Asbury, music was the preferred form of artistic expression, and she became an accomplished violinist.

No written record remains of Asbury's experiences at Penn, and only sketchy details can be gleaned from family papers housed at Howard University. But there is a charming photo of her, violin tucked under her arm and an expression of utter self-confidence upon her face, that speaks volumes. Upon graduation, she taught music and in 1901 married John Cornelius Asbury, a Harvard-educated lawyer who would go on to became a state legislator, Republican leader of Philadelphia's 30th ward, and the first African-American assistant district attorney in Philadelphia.

Although she never stopped teaching music, and arranged many musical programs through her affiliation with the interracial Episcopalian Church of the Crucifixion in Philadelphia, Asbury directed much of her energy into managing the Home for Aged and Infirmed Colored Persons in West Philadelphia (later called the Stephen Smith Home).

In 1926, both she and her husband were selected by Philadelphia's Mayor W. Freeland Kendrick to serve on the committee in charge of Negro activities for the Sesquicentennial International Exposition. A few years later, she made an extended trip to Europe for travel and study.

Asbury seems to have led a simple life, one of cultural opportunity and service to her community. Her remarkable achievement is that it all seems so utterly unremarkable — until you remember the double obstacles of race and gender that she quietly transcended.

Anna Lindsay

When she was 13, Anna Robertson Brown Lindsay began taking classes in counterpoint and music at the University of Pennsylvania. She was just 19 when she graduated from Wellesley College, and only 28 when she received a Ph.D., the first woman to earn that degree from the University of Pennsylvania.

She never stopped to rest on her academic laurels. In 1893, at the age of 29, Lindsay published the first in a series of phenomenally successful inspirational books that were immediate best sellers. That first book, *What Is Worth While?*, was actually written as a paper for a philosophy course she had taken ten years earlier at Wellesley. It sold more than 400,000 copies, was translated into Arabic and Japanese, and stayed in print for 62 years. The book's opening lines give a good sense of Lindsay's style and an even better sense of the almost feverish energy that enabled her to post so many accomplishments so quickly: "Only one life to live! We all want to do our best with it. We all want to make the most of it. How can we best get hold of it? How can we accomplish the most with the energies and powers at our command? What is worth while?"

Lindsay was born in Washington, D.C., during the Civil War to Dr. William Y. Brown, a Presbyterian minister, and Flora Robertson Brown. She attended public and private schools in Philadelphia and enrolled in classes at Penn for two years ("At the insistent request of the Professor

Born: 1864 Died: 1948

18

of Music, who was my piano and organ teacher," she writes). Entering Wellesley as a sophomore in 1880, she received her bachelor's degree in 1883 and taught college preparatory courses at the Wellesley Preparatory School in Philadelphia before moving to England to pursue further study at Oxford University in 1887.

Returning to Philadelphia in 1889, she enrolled in Penn's graduate philosophy department and received her doctorate in 1892. Within a year, Lindsay published her first book and over the course of the next 31 years produced 34 inspirational works that found an avid market.

In 1896 she married Dr. Samuel McCune Lindsay, a professor of sociology at Penn who later became a distinguished sociologist at Columbia University, but neither marriage nor the ensuing birth of three children seemed to diminish Lindsay's literary output. At the same time, she kept up an active involvement in a number of educational and charitable organizations, including Phi Beta Kappa, the Association of Collegiate Alumnae, and the American Association of University Women. She served as a trustee of Wellesley College and was a member of its Alumnae Association Council for 14 years. Together with her husband, who was responsible for drafting child labor laws for President Theodore Roosevelt, she founded the University of Puerto Rico. In 1924, at the age of 60, she traveled to Lima, Peru, to attend the Pan-

American Congress of Women and in the following year was made an honorary member of the Comite Internacional de Universitarias Graduadas in Peru. For 62 years Lindsay taught Sunday school in the various Presbyterian churches where she held membership.

She was modest to a fault. In autobiographical comments written for Wellesley in her later years, Lindsay listed her occupations, in the following order, as "wife, mother, author." In a later version, written shortly before she died, Lindsay added that homemaking "has always been my basic married occupation, but complementary to it I have had much reading, study, writing, interesting outside engagements, travel, and association with my husband's work and affiliations."

In *Giving What We Have,* published in 1897, the year her first child was born, Lindsay writes: "If we fritter away our lives, we may go down to the grave with but this epitaph above us: To the millions that have lived, he added one. He made one more." She then adds a consoling sentiment that could easily be read as her guiding philosophy in life: "No real work falls to the ground. What God means you or me to do is not a waste of force. There is in all the universe no lost power. The labor of our hands, the steps of our feet, the burden of our backs, shall all pass into the final sum of our gifts to men."

Mary Pennington

*F*resh fruit in February, pure milk in August, eggs that are sanitary for holiday baking, and butchered meat that won't sicken your guests.

We take these things for granted now. But our ancestors couldn't 100 years ago when a young bacteriological chemist turned her considerable energy and intellect to solving the problem of storing and transporting perishable goods in this country.

Mary Engle Pennington was born just after the Civil War in Nashville, Tenn., to Quaker parents Henry Pennington and Sarah B. Molony. Soon after her birth, the family moved to Philadelphia to be closer to Sarah's Quaker roots. Those roots, and a deep affection for the city that nourished them all, remained with Mary Pennington all her life.

Her affinity for science surfaced early. In a 1941 *New Yorker* profile, Pennington recalled whiling away hot summer afternoons at the age of 12 reading a text on medical chemistry. Halfway through the chapter on nitrogen and oxygen she made a crucial connection. "Suddenly, one day," she is quoted as saying, "I realized, lickity hoop, that although I couldn't touch, taste, or smell them they really existed. It was a milestone."

Another milestone was persuading the dean at the University of Pennsylvania to allow her to enroll, at the age of 15, in what was then the Towne Scientific School. After three years studying chemistry and biology, Pennington was eligible for a bachelor of science degree. This was denied her because of her sex, and she was instead awarded a certificate of proficiency. But under an old University statute allowing for exceptions in "extraordinary cases," Pennington was allowed to stay on and work towards a Ph.D. The caveat: she could not apply for the degree until she came of age. She waited until 22, then received her doctorate, with a major in chemistry and minors in zoology and botany.

Her studies completed, Pennington focused her energies in an entrepreneurial direction. Signing up 400 Philadelphia physicians as subscribing customers for bacteriological analysis, she and fellow Penn graduate Elizabeth Atkinson successfully established themselves as the Philadelphia Clinical Laboratory. It was only a short time before city fathers bowed to the obvious and asked her to head up the Philadelphia Department of Health and Charities Bacteriological Laboratory. There Pennington tackled the problem of impure milk and milk products in the city. Of particular concern was the hokeypokey ice cream sold by push-cart vendors, mostly to children in the city's poorer neighborhoods. By showing the peddlers microscopic slides of the various unsavory organisms swarming through their products, Pennington effectively persuaded them to boil their pots and ladles. Her research also led to a detailed analysis of the preservation of milk at low temperatures and the science of refrigeration.

With the passage of the U.S. Pure Food and Drug Act in 1906, Pennington was asked by a family friend to take the civil service examination for chief of the Food Research Laboratory of the U.S. Department of Agriculture. Reluctantly she agreed, unaware that she was enrolled for the exam as M.E. Pennington. She nailed the exam and was offered the job before examiners realized she was a woman. As chief of the laboratory, Pennington developed a technique for the slaughter of poultry and the treatment of egg products that revolutionized the industry.

With the advent of World War I, Pennington moved in a new direction. As part of a team investigating refrigeration conditions for perishable cargoes in railroad cars, Pennington criss-crossed the country 500 times. Using her data, the Department of Agriculture laid down industrywide standards for refrigerator car ventilation and insulation. The only woman in a 28-man unit that called themselves "The Imperishables," Pennington earned misplaced notoriety for reportedly traveling entirely by refrigerator car. In fact, she had done nothing of the sort, living instead in the relative comfort of the caboose. More deserved was her Notable Service Medal, awarded in 1919 by Herbert Hoover, then director of the War Food Administration.

In the years between the wars, Pennington turned her talents to consulting. In that capacity she spread the gospel of refrigeration far and wide, authoring numerous pamphlets on food and food preservation, including the memorably titled "Journeys with Refrigerated Food" and "The Romance of Ice."

The first female member of the American Society of Refrigerating Engineers, and one of the first female members of the American Chemical Society, Pennington was hailed at her death in 1953 as one of the nation's outstanding food and refrigeration scientists.

But her legacy extends beyond the confines of the scientific community. Cooks in kitchens throughout the nation have been awakened to the dangers of unchecked salmonella and other food-borne illnesses. We unthinkingly enjoy the fruits of her research every time we are able to bring a healthy meal from freezer to table in 20 minutes or less. And we are grateful for the beneficence of strawberries in February.

Margaret Klingelsmith

*M*argaret Center Klingelsmith was one of the early beneficiaries of Carrie Burnham Kilgore's lengthy crusade to have women admitted to the Pennsylvania bar. She knew Kilgore and corresponded with her. But Klingelsmith's style was different, and she preferred research, scholarship, and the hush of the library to the thrust and dash of courtroom litigation.

Both Klingelsmith's parents, Isaac Henry Center and Carolina How Evans, came from prominent New England families. Born in Portland, Maine, Klingelsmith was educated in private schools in Maine and Massachusetts. She married Joseph Klingelsmith in 1884 in Atlanta, Ga., but in 1893 migrated to Philadelphia and entered the law offices of William Draper Lewis, future dean of the University of Pennsylvania Law School. After two years of study with Lewis, Klingelsmith enrolled as a sophomore at Penn.

She graduated in 1898 and was admitted to the bar that same year, the second or third woman to take advantage of Kilgore's victory. Yet in 1899, when she was appointed librarian of the Biddle Law Library (a position she was to hold for the next 32 years), Klingelsmith happily forsook the courts to pursue an increasingly distinguished career as a legal librarian, writer, and scholar.

At the time of her appointment, the law library contained fewer than 10,000 volumes. Under Klingelsmith's direction, which included several buying trips to Europe where she ferreted out rare and valuable books, the library expanded more than elevenfold, boasting 82,000 volumes and a national reputation by the time of her death in 1931.

Klingelsmith also authored biographies of U.S. Chief Justice John Marshall, Jeremiah Sullivan Black, and James Wilson, founder of Penn's law school and a signer of the Declaration of Independence. But her magnum opus was the painstaking translation of Statham's *Digest*, the earliest compilation of common law, written in an abbreviated Norman-French language with no pagination and obscure citations. The work took more than four years to complete. In recognition of this achievement, Penn awarded her an honorary master of laws degree in 1916, the first such given to a woman.

While committed to a more scholarly career than Kilgore, Klingelsmith remained a strong advocate for women entering the legal profession. She taught a free class in municipal law through the Woman's Sanitary League of Pennsylvania and opened the Biddle Law Library for free lectures and classes for women interested in entering the profession.

And she didn't shirk confrontation. In 1901, Klingelsmith allowed her name to be put forward for membership in Philadelphia's all-male Law Academy. "As far as I am personally concerned, membership in the Academy will be of no great advantage," she is quoted in Philadelphia's *Bulletin*. "But to have its doors thrown open to my sex will materially aid all women students."

When her membership was rejected — on the grounds that it would set a bad precedent — Klingelsmith accepted defeat gracefully and moved on. Active in suffrage activities and the Democratic Party, Klingelsmith wrote numerous letters, speeches, and pamphlets in support of both. She joined Alice Paul as one of the speakers at Philadelphia's first open-air meeting for women's suffrage in 1911. The meeting, although unpublicized to avoid police action, attracted a crowd of 300 whose orderly behavior helped Klingelsmith and Paul avoid incarceration for illegal assembly.

Klingelsmith infused all of her efforts with quiet wit and sharp reasoning. Writing in 1911 on the issue of whether clothes make the man (or woman), Klingelsmith invoked portraits of the nation's Founding Fathers and reasoned, "If ruffles and frills and silks and velvets mean weakmindedness surely our republic should have fallen before this."

When she was awarded her honorary degree from Penn, Klingelsmith cautioned a reporter against thinking that the legal profession held limited opportunities for women. "A man once told me that he thought the day would come when men will do all the pleading at the courts, and women will do all the office work," Klingelsmith said, adding, "No, that isn't a slur by any means. It is a compliment, for it is the office work that is really the thinking work, and women are just as good thinkers as men."

Alice Paul

When Alice Paul came to the University of Pennsylvania in 1906 to study for her master's degree in sociology, she was looking for direction. By the time she departed from the University in 1912 as a newly minted doctor of philosophy, she had found her cause — equal rights for women — and gained the skills to pursue it relentlessly for the rest of her life.

Paul was born in Moorestown, N.J., in 1885, to William Paul and Tacie Parry, prosperous and devout Quakers. At the age of 16, Paul enrolled in Swarthmore College, the same school her mother had attended. Graduating in 1905, Paul went to New York for an internship in social work. She earned a diploma from the New York School of Social Work in 1906, but the experience convinced her that individual social work was not for her. "I knew in a very short time I was never going to be a social worker," Paul recalled in an oral history taken in old age. "You knew you couldn't change the situation by social work."

In 1907, Paul received her master's degree from Penn and a Quaker scholarship to study in England. There she became involved in the British suffrage movement, and was arrested numerous times for civil disobedience. While in jail she went on hunger strikes and like many of her colleagues was brutally force-fed through nasal feeding tubes.

Although committed to her cause, Paul was very concerned that her Quaker family would misunderstand her actions. In a letter written to her mother in 1909 after she was released from one of her prison stays, Paul admitted, "I am sorry thee was so worried. I thought thee might be, so I decided to not let thee know I had gone until I came out."

It was more than the Quakers who minded her tactics. When Paul returned to Philadelphia in 1911, local suffragist groups who deplored the militance of their British sisters treated her gingerly. But for Paul, who had been revolutionized by her experiences in England, there was no turning back.

Ellery Stowall, Paul's doctoral supervisor at Penn, remembered her as a brilliant student who was focused entirely on one goal: "She wanted the degree so that none might question her preparation and training when she came before committees in her support of the women's movement," recalled Stowall. "She had a fine taste in dress, but when one of her friends admired the hat she was wearing she gave it to her and went about in a much less becoming substitute. It seemed to be a matter of supreme indifference to her, lost as she was in lifting the lowly condition of women throughout this world."

While completing her studies, Paul helped organize Philadelphia's first open-air suffrage rallies in the summer of 1911, joining, among others, Penn law librarian Margaret Klingelsmith. Recognizing the publicity value of her experiences, Paul frequently spoke about her incarcerations in England.

By the time she graduated with her doctorate in 1912 (her dissertation was "Towards Equality: The Legal Position of Women in Pennsylvania") Paul was convinced that women needed to pursue the right to vote through a federal amendment to the Constitution rather than pushing for it state by state. In 1913 she assumed control of the Congressional Committee of the National American Woman Suffrage Association (NAWSA) with Lucy Burns, a fellow American suffragist who had been in England with Paul. Within months of her appointment, she organized a parade of 5,000 suffragists to march though Washington on the eve of President Woodrow Wilson's inauguration. The march drew the attention of the press and derision from the crowd, but it also alarmed NAWSA leaders, who were fearful that Paul's higher-profile tactics would harm their cause.

Within three years, Paul and Burns broke with NAWSA and formed the more militant National Women's Party. It was this group that initiated 24-hour pickets at the White House, silent sentinels demanding the president's attention. For their efforts, many, including Paul, were jailed and subjected to conditions as brutal as those Paul had endured in England. But the suffragists managed to leak word about the conditions, orchestrating a public backlash against their mistreatment.

When Congress passed the 19th Amendment in 1919, Paul immediately turned her attention towards drafting an Equal Rights Amendment (ERA), even attending law school in Washington to enhance her legislative knowledge. The campaign for an ERA was to consume the rest of Paul's life, although she also took time in 1938 to establish the World Woman's Party and was instrumental in placing the principle of women's equal rights within the charter of the United Nations.

A journalist in 1919 wrote of Paul, "There is no Alice Paul. She leads by being ... her cause."

When she graduated from Penn in 1912, Paul had a photo taken of herself in full academic regalia. Attached prominently to her academic hood is the prison door pin that was created by British suffragists for those who had been jailed fighting for the right to vote. The symbolism is fitting. Paul devoted her life to opening doors for women. Supporting her in that determination were the academic gifts she received from Benjamin Franklin's university.

Alice Paul celebrates passage of the 19th Amendment.

Sadie Alexander

Born: 1898 Died: 1989

What must it have been like to be the first African-American woman in this country to receive a doctorate in economics? To be the first to receive a law degree from the University of Pennsylvania? To be the first admitted to the Pennsylvania bar? What must it have been like to be invisible? "You spoke perfect English, but no one spoke to you," Saddie Mossell Alexander wrote of her experience at Penn. "Can you imagine looking for classrooms and asking persons the way, only to find the same unresponsive persons you asked for directions seated in the classroom, which you entered late because you could not find your way? Just suppose that after finding your way to a seat in the classroom, not one person spoke to you."

Alexander was born in Philadelphia, to a family accustomed to breaking down barriers. Her father, Aaron Mossell, was the first African-American graduate of Penn's law school, and her uncle, Nathan Mossell, was the first African-American graduate of Penn's medical school. Alexander's mother, Mary Tanner, was the daughter of Benjamin Tucker Tanner, a bishop in the African Methodist Episcopal Church, and the sister of the painter Henry O. Tanner, one of whose paintings now hangs in the White House.

Because her father deserted the family when Alexander was young, she divided her childhood between Philadelphia and Washington, D.C. In 1915 she enrolled in the School of Education at the University of Pennsylvania, graduated in three years, and immediately embarked on a graduate degree in economics. Although her doctoral dissertation (on the spending patterns of African-American migrant families in Philadelphia) was published in the *Annals of the American Academy of Political and Social Sciences,* Alexander herself was forced to migrate for employment after she received her doctorate in 1921.

Moving to Durham, N.C., she became an actuary for an African-American firm, the North Carolina Mutual Life Insurance Co. In 1923 she married Raymond Pace Alexander, a fellow Penn economist and a graduate of Harvard Law School, and moved back to Philadelphia. "Well, I stayed home for one year and almost lost my mind," she recalled. "You know, in those days it would have been impossible had I wanted to teach because blacks were not being hired for any high school positions, and the only jobs available were in black elementary schools. So I decided to go to law school."

There she found her true calling. One of the top students in her class, she was chosen to help edit the law review (against the wishes of Dean Edward Mikell, who personally blocked her appointment, backing down only when Law Review Editor Philip Werner Amram threatened to resign). Graduating with honors in 1927, she went into practice with her husband and soon thereafter became the first African-American woman to work in the Philadelphia city solicitor's office.

Even while pursuing a burgeoning law career and raising two daughters, Alexander never forgot her early experiences. She and her husband threw themselves into civil rights work, drafting antisegregation laws — including the 1935 Pennsylvania Public Accommodations Act that desegregated Philadelphia restaurants, hotels, and theaters — and filing court cases to test their enforcement. As founding members of the John Mercer Langston Law Club, formed in 1925 when African-Americans were excluded from the Philadelphia Bar Association, the Alexanders were also instrumental in setting up a legal aid bureau to help those who were unable to afford legal assistance. Alexander was also responsible for the creation of Philadelphia's Human Relations Commission and in 1952 became one its first commissioners.

"Raymond and I agreed, as far back as when he was an aspiring law student, that we would break up the problems plaguing black people in Philadelphia as soon as we had completed our educations," Alexander wrote. "And we both did just that."

In recognition of her work in civil rights, Alexander was appointed to President Truman's Committee on Civil Rights in 1946. In 1963, President Kennedy appointed her to his Lawyer's Committee for Civil Rights and Law, and in 1979 President Carter tapped her to chair the White House Conference on Aging.

By the time she received Penn's Distinguished Service Award in 1980, one thing was abundantly clear: Sadie Alexander was no longer invisible.

Gladys Tantaquidgeon

In the spiritual tradition of Connecticut's Mohegan Indians, Granny Squannit is a beloved intermediary between the Mohegan people and woodland spirits. In return for small gifts of food left in the forest, Granny shares knowledge of the medicinal properties of herbs and plants with the tribe's medicine women. "She performs the function of allotting to humans a share of her domain of blessings," explains Mohegan medicine woman Gladys Tantaquidgeon, "Squannit exercises beneficent care not only for the material needs of the Indians but for their spiritual requirements..."

So, it seems, has Tantaquidgeon, Granny Squannit's spiritual heir. Her life's work as the guardian of Mohegan heritage was pivotal in the restoration of tribal status to her people in 1994. At the age of 102, Tantaquidgeon is now witness to a dramatic resurgence in tribal pride and prosperity that is the direct result of her work both as an anthropologist working within her own community and as that community's cultural treasurer.

"Remember to take the best of what the white man has to offer," she once counseled, "and use it to still be an Indian."

She's done it, and her tribe has followed. With profits from its Mohegan Sun casino, opened in 1997 after tribal status was established, the Mohegans have been able to fund college scholarships of $20,000 a year to any young Mohegan who graduates from high school, to build a new home for tribal elderly, to underwrite a campaign to reclaim artifacts from outside museum collections, and, most recently, to donate $1 million to the Twin Towers fund assisting families of victims of the Sept. 11 terrorist attacks in New York.

Born: 1899

Tantaquidgeon was born to John and Harriet Fielding Tantaquidgeon in Montville, Conn., just before the turn of the last century. From an early age she was fascinated by tribal customs and attached herself particularly to three older women, who repaid her curiosity and interest with gentle tuition. Although only one was her true grandmother (the other two were aunts), Tantaquidgeon called all of them "nanu" and spent most of her childhood in their company, identifying and collecting medicinal herbs, listening to stories, and absorbing her heritage. "My maternal grandmother taught me most of what I learned," Tantaquidgeon said, "I don't recall if I had any books or not."

Tantaquidgeon came to the attention of anthropologist Dr. Frank Speck, who first began studying the Mohegan and other New England tribes while a student at Columbia University. Delighted with the precocious young girl, Speck, who went on to found the University of Pennsylvania's Department of Anthropology, included her in his field studies of East Coast Indians. At the age of 20, Tantaquidgeon came to Penn as an assistant to Speck.

With no high school diploma, Tantaquidgeon did not enter a degree program at the University. But over the course of the next several years, she attended classes in Penn's College Courses for Teachers program, a precursor to the College of General Studies. During this time, Tantaquidgeon also did field work with Speck, transcribing notes and traveling frequently with him to meet representatives of Eastern Indian tribes.

While at Penn, Tantaquidgeon stayed either with Speck and his wife in suburban Swarthmore or roomed with another Speck protégé, Penobscot Indian Molly Dellis Nelson, at the University's International House.

The two women cut their long braids into flapper bobs and wore their beaded belts slung low on their hips in the style of the 1920s but never lost their Indian identity. In 1925, Tantaquidgeon participated with other Native Americans in a special Music League of Philadelphia pageant at Franklin Field.

In 1934, Speck recommended Tantaquidgeon for a community worker position with the Bureau of Indian Affairs. She was sent first to Maine then to the Yankton Sioux Reservation in South Dakota, doing social work there as the bureau's first Native American specialist for two years before taking a job with the newly formed Federal Indian Arts and Crafts Board.

Through this agency, Tantaquidgeon assisted Lakota Sioux throughout the West in creating and displaying traditional crafts, bringing much-needed revenue into the reservations and at the same time preserving skills that had been handed down for generations.

In 1947, Tantaquidgeon brought her anthropological skills home to Connecticut, assisting her father and brother with the running of a Mohegan museum the family had started in 1931, and immersing herself in traditional tribal activities.

"I feel that I like to take part in and appreciate my heritage," Tantaquidgeon said, "and perhaps pass along a few survivals to not only our younger generations, but to other people who are interested."

Many were, and generations of children who visited the Tantaquidgeon Museum in school and scouting groups learned from its gentle curator the same stories and customs that captured her own imagination as a child.

It was this compendium of knowledge, much of it written and published by Tantaquidgeon in scholarly papers and journals, along with documents and artifacts she collected over a lifetime of research, that ultimately convinced federal authorities to grant Mohegans their status as a sovereign Indian nation in 1994.

The designation, as far as Tantaquidgeon was concerned, was never in doubt. "One thing about Gladys is that she's an eternal optimist," says Melissa Fawcett, Tantaquidgeon's great-niece and Mohegan tribal historian. "She gave people the strength to believe in who they were."

Sister Constance Murphy

*I*t's not easy to pigeon-hole Sister Constance Murphy. An African-American Anglican nun, she is a Baltimore native who has lived for years in Canada. A devoted teacher, she switched to a successful second career in gerontology at about the age when most of her cohort was retiring.

"All my life I've been lucky," Murphy says of her experiences. "I've been presented with many changes."

Luck, you might say, has nothing to do with it. Murphy embraces change with the same enthusiasm that she embraces life. Life, it seems, just returns the favor.

Born just after the turn of the last century, Murphy was the third child and second daughter of Grace Lee Hughes Murphy and George Benjamin Murphy, whose roots in Baltimore's community of African-American professionals extended back several generations. Her paternal grandfather, John H. Murphy Sr., was the founder and editor of the *AFRO-American* newspaper. Her maternal grandfather, James Hughes, ran a well-known catering business in the city.

Education was important in Murphy's family, but Murphy's five brothers were given first dibs at attending college. Murphy and her sister enrolled in the Baltimore Normal School and after graduation took up teaching careers. Murphy enrolled for two summer sessions at the University of Pennsylvania before finally taking a two-year break from teaching to finish her degree. She says she chose Penn because an aunt had taken summer courses there and recommended the pro-

Born: 1904

gram. And it was comparatively close to home. But there was another reason: "Back then," Murphy says, "Johns Hopkins and the University of Maryland didn't welcome colored students."

Even at Penn, Murphy's race set her somewhat apart. But she took it in stride. She recalls the first day of a class called "The Irish Experience" taught by Dr. Frank Allan Laurie. When he came to her name while calling the roll he said, "Oh, yes! There's an Irish lassie. Where are you?" And she stood up. "Well, if you could have seen his face," Murphy says, "He didn't expect a colored girl." Laurie went on to become a good friend, eventually heading up the interracial club.

Murphy packed as much college experience as she could into her two years on campus, playing intramural field hockey and joining Delta Sigma Theta, a sorority that her aunt had started. Upon graduation in 1928, having earned a bachelor's degree in education, she returned to Baltimore to pick up her teaching career.

But while she enjoyed teaching, Murphy found herself searching for something more. Hearing a church presentation about the work of the Toronto-based Sisterhood of St. John the Divine, the first Anglican women's community in Canada, Murphy was intrigued. She asked for more information, and after several trips to visit the mother house in Canada, Murphy opted for another change in her life. In 1932 she moved north to test her vocation.

"My family was against my going into the order," Murphy recalls. "I was moving so far away, and they wanted me to marry and have children." But as far as she was concerned, Murphy says, "This was what I wanted." After taking her final vows, Murphy began tutoring special education students in Toronto. In 1938 she moved out to Qu'Appelle Diocesan School in Saskatchewan. Murphy spent 17 years at the school, eventually rising to the position of headmistress.

When she returned to Toronto in 1955, however, a new career beckoned. Taking up a position as administrator of the Church Home for the Aged, Murphy quickly turned her attention to the nascent field of gerontology. In addition to running the home, Murphy was involved in a number of projects related to the aging, including the publication of a volume of prayers and hymns in large print.

A founding member of both the Diocese of Toronto's Committee on the Elderly and the Canadian Institute of Religion and Gerontology, Murphy served as Canadian observer to three White House Conferences on Aging, attending her first one at the invitation of fellow Penn alumna Sadie Mossell Alexander. In 1976, at the age of 72, she returned to college, graduating a year later from the University of Michigan with a master's in adult education and a certificate in gerontology. As an outgrowth of her interest in aging, Murphy became one of the first women to participate in the Baltimore Longitudinal Study of Aging, the country's longest-running scientific study of human aging.

Murphy still keeps busy, regularly visiting elderly parishioners of St.Hilda's Church in Toronto, several of them younger than herself. Visiting Penn in 1993 for her 65th college reunion, Murphy spurned riding a golf cart in the class parade, preferring instead to walk. She published her memoirs in 1997, and has plans to write a book on gerontology.

It amuses her to ponder the growth of educational opportunities for women, but Murphy doubts, given the option, that she would choose a career path markedly different from the one she took. "All good teachers," she remarks, "are great helpers."

Her comment amplifies an earlier admission in her book: "I was then, and still am, I think, not just a doer, but a doer about something."

Ruth Klein

hen Laura Ruth Murray Klein entered Penn as a freshman in the fall of 1927, she was one of 125 women enrolled in the School of Education — the only school at the University at the time open to full-time female students.

Education may have been one of the few career choices available, but it's hard to imagine Klein doing anything different. For 41 years, she worked for the Philadelphia School District, a career that culminated in her appointment as principal of Girls' High, the city's magnet school for academically gifted young women whose graduates include, among others, Penn President Judith Rodin.

Klein, who was born in 1910 to Robert Murray, a mortgage and real estate officer at the Philadelphia Savings Fund Society, and Laura Mosebach Murray, commuted to Penn her first year, like most of her classmates. Yet even in a campus atmosphere that wasn't particularly welcoming to women, Klein flourished.

"I used to sit in the front row because then I didn't feel queer asking questions," Klein recalled in an oral history taken in 1988. "I definitely liked doing it." That same willingness to put herself forward gained her a berth as the only freshman woman on the debate team (and the resulting advantage of being allowed on the second floor of Houston Hall). She competed for three years on the team, eventually serving as team captain and manager.

A member of Chi Omega sorority, as well as the Glee and Drama

Clubs, Klein graduated Phi Beta Kappa in 1931 with a degree in education. She received her master's degree in 1933 and her doctorate in education ten years later in 1943.

She was an educator all her life. She taught English and drama at Olney and Germantown High Schools and South Philadelphia High School for Boys. In 1952, she moved into administration when she was appointed vice principal of Bartram High School, becoming principal of Tilden High School in 1957.

Coming to Girls' High was the capstone to Klein's career, and she stayed in that position for 13 years, from 1963 until her retirement in 1976. They were momentous times — anti-war protests, hippies, radical feminism, new educational mandates. Yet Klein (and Girls' High) weathered them with patient grace.

"It's not only a question of having a relevant education, but of making people aware of what is relevant and what is not — and keeping a sort of balance between experimenting and holding to certain ideas which have proved valuable over time," Klein explained in a 1972 interview. "It's also a question of giving the students the opportunity to look at themselves both as individuals and as part of a larger group, and to realize that sometimes one has to be important, sometimes the other."

Among her initiatives at Girls' High was the Study-Action in Philadelphia Program that sent seniors out into the community on internships. Klein also helped introduce extra electives to the school's curriculum, including child development, fencing, modern Hebrew culture and civilization, computer programming, and yoga. And she personally signed the diploma of every girl who graduated during her tenure.

Despite her busy career and home life (Klein married attorney Randolph Klein in 1934; widowed young, she raised their two children as a single mother), she remained active in the Penn community as well. She organized and chaired Alumnae for Annual Giving, worked on the committee that reorganized alumni groups at the University, and later served as one of the first directors of the General Alumni Society. The first woman to receive the Alumni Award of Merit, Klein also served as president of the Philadelphia chapter of the American Association of University Women.

In retirement, Klein maintained an interest in education, becoming chairman and president of Philadelphia's Please Touch Museum. And she never truly left the classroom. For 49 years she taught Sunday school to children at Oak Lane Presbyterian Church in Philadelphia. To them, as to many of her friends, Klein was known as Patsy. Her old classroom at the church now bears an official designation on its wall: "Patsy's Room."

Althea Hottel

Born: 1907 Died: 2000

*A*gainst the strong wishes of family and friends, Althea Kratz Hottel chose to go to the University of Pennsylvania.

Their objections were familiar: Penn was a man's institution, and the men there were not happy about women joining them on campus.

"I had been told by men this was no place for women. They were second-class citizens," Hottel recalled in an address she gave in 1975 marking the 100th anniversary of women at Penn. But she was undeterred: "I opted for quality education."

Hottel was born in 1907 to Clarence Markley Kratz, a treasurer at Eastern State Penitentiary, and Nettie Hallowel Kratz. Even in high school Hottel displayed the extraordinary drive and energy that marked her throughout her life. As valedictorian of her class at Lansdale High School, she posted the highest grades in the school's history.

When Hottel enrolled at Penn in 1925 as an education major, there were no women teachers except in physical education. Until her senior year, she did not have men in any of her classes. And many programs within the University were not open to women. In an oral history conducted after her retirement, Hottel recalled that women who wanted to major in biology or pre-med had to take those classes at odd times — in the evening or on Saturday. And there were still some members of the faculty who made it clear they didn't want any women in their classes.

Unfortunately, it wasn't just the men who made life miserable for freshman women. Sophomore women hazed the new students unmercifully, Hottel remembered, requiring them to spout off school songs and other information from the freshman handbook by heart. Yet by the time she herself was a sophomore, Hottel had become a leader in the strong — if separate — community that women formed within the larger University. Women had their own student government (the Women's Student Government Association, or WSGA) and their own activities such as undergraduate stunt nights and teas in Sergeant Hall presided over by Genie Crawford, the directress of women (who also hosted May Day celebrations for women students at her country estate). Because nearly all the women, Hottel included, commuted to class and lived at home, an active sorority system gave women students a base on campus. Hottel pledged Tri Delta, finding there a lively and welcoming community.

It is exhausting just to read about Hottel's many accomplishments as an undergraduate. She was junior-year president of her class, president of the WSGA in her senior year, and a cabinet member of the women's division of the Christian Association. She was elected a member of the Sphinx and Key, Mortar Board, and Pi Lambda Theta honor societies, and voted "most popular," "hardest worker," and "best all-around girl" by her classmates.

"We'd like to say more about Althea, but really, we never see anything of her, for she's always off to some convention or other for WSGA," reported sorority sister Muriel Morton in the March 1929, issue of Tri Delta's national magazine, *Trident*. "With all this and a lot of other things on her extremely capable shoulders," Morton continued, "Althea very nonchalantly gets D's in everything!" (D—standing for distinguished—was the highest grade achievable at Penn.)

It is safe to assume Morton was exaggerating that last part.

During her summers, Hottel participated as a counselor in the University Camp for Girls run by Penn's Christian Association. The camp, located at Green Lane to the northwest of campus, provided local underprivileged youth, many of them residents of the University Settlement House, with a summer away from hot city streets. For Hottel, it confirmed her desire to make a career in education.

After graduating from Penn in 1929, she spent one year as a high school teacher and another on staff at Penn's graduate hospital before returning to pursue a graduate degree. In 1936, while still working towards her Ph.D. in sociology (she received the degree in 1940), Hottel became Penn's directress of women, a position that seven years later was renamed dean of women. She held the job for the next 23 years, leaving an indelible mark on the newly created College for Women and the University as a whole.

Among her many accomplishments as dean of women was the opening of all schools within the University to women students, the creation of a women's student union on the top floor of Bennett Hall, and, finally, spearheading fundraising and support for the construction of the first women's dormitory on campus, Hill Hall.

Although she retired as dean and instructor in sociology in 1959 to spend more time with her husband, Abram Hottel, Jr., whom she had married in 1945, Hottel continued to remain active in the university community, serving from 1959-1969 as the University's second woman trustee. In her honor, the University in 1959 established the Althea Kratz Hottel Award as the first senior honor award for women.

When she graduated in 1929, Hottel's class predicted she would become the first woman president of the United States. Fortunately for Penn, she channeled her prodigious energy closer to home, creating an educational environment that continues to nurture succeeding generations of women leaders.

Jessie Scott

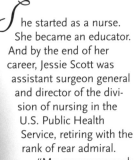

Born: 1915

She started as a nurse. She became an educator. And by the end of her career, Jessie Scott was assistant surgeon general and director of the division of nursing in the U.S. Public Health Service, retiring with the rank of rear admiral.

"My career was probably laid out to me in the very beginning," says Scott, who was born in Wilkes-Barre, Pa., shortly before the First World War to Chester and Eva Snyder Scott. Two of her paternal aunts were nurses. And when Scott, who had contracted rheumatic fever as an infant, entered grade school, she recalls being fascinated with the school nurse who took a special interest in her health.

In 1936, Scott graduated from Wilkes-Barre General Hospital Training School for Nurses. It was the middle of the Depression, and Scott did private practice nursing for several years before enrolling in a new program at the University of Pennsylvania that allowed registered nurses to pursue bachelor's degrees through the School of Education. Scott was attracted to the program because of its dean, Katherine Tucker, a public health nurse who had formerly served as executive director of the National Organization of Public Health Nursing in New York. Recruited by Penn to set up its fledgling program in 1935, "Dr. Tucker was a tremendous asset," says Scott, noting, "She brought the nursing world to the school."

Graduating in three years with a bachelor's degree in nursing education, Scott became educational director of the Mount Sinai Hospital School of Nursing in Philadelphia where she also taught anatomy to students preparing for wartime nursing duty.

At the end of the war, Scott moved to New York to pursue a master's degree in personnel administration at Columbia University. In 1949, with her degree in hand, Scott turned her attention from strict science to social science, becoming a career counselor for the Professional Counseling and Placement Service of the Pennsylvania Nurses Association. The program was part of a nationwide initiative to provide assistance to the 75,000 nurse veterans seeking to further their education and improve their job prospects after the war. In that position, Scott worked both with nurses and with employers looking to fill positions.

In 1955 Scott joined the U.S. Public Health Service's Division of Nursing. Initially, she says, she planned to stay in that job for only a few years and then go back to Penn to finish her doctorate. She never did, and Penn's loss was the nation's gain.

Starting as a consultant, Scott rose quickly to become director of the division. She traveled the globe observing and advising on nursing education programs in countries such as India, Egypt, Liberia, and Kenya. She spent two winter months in Alaska studying the provision of health care to native peoples living on the Bering Sea, and several weeks in China observing that country's barefoot doctors, who provided basic health care in isolated rural communities. For several years, Scott was a member of an international seminar sponsored by King's Fund College in London, and she participated as a faculty member in a trans-Pacific nursing conference with Australia and New Zealand.

It was important work. But Scott is most proud of her involvement in a more domestic initiative: the 1964 Nurse Training Act. The outgrowth of recommendations from the nursing profession, the act funded improvements in nursing school curriculum, student scholarships and loans, the development of nurse practitioner programs, and the construction and updating of facilities to include research laboratories in nursing schools around the country.

"It was the first major piece of legislation providing support for nursing in peacetime," Scott says. Of the resulting program, which she administered from its inception until her retirement in 1979, Scott proudly notes: "With the legislation, the budget, and the support we had, we were able to move nursing education forward. It represented a great boost for nursing in this country."

Among the beneficiaries was the University of Pennsylvania, which used Nurse Training Act funds to construct the building that currently houses its School of Nursing.

Dubbed a Living Legend by the American Academy of Nursing, Scott is the recipient of 16 honorary degrees, including one conferred by Penn in 1983. Among other awards, she is the recipient of a distinguished service medal from the U.S. Public Health Service, the National League of Nursing's Nutting Award for national and international leadership, Columbia University's McManus Medal for leadership, a Mentor Award from Sigma Theta Tau, the honorary nursing society, and the Spirit of Nursing Award given on the 100th anniversary of the Visiting Nurse Society of New York City. The American Nurses Association administers the biannual Jessie M. Scott Leadership Award, and the University of Maryland, the site of a graduate program in nursing and health policy that Scott set up when she retired from the Public Health Service, offers the Jessie M. Scott Health Policy Award each year to a nurse who has distinguished herself in the field.

Throughout her career in the Public Health Service, Scott frequently testified before Congress in defense of the division's program. She was, she says, most appreciative of the opportunity.

"I'm convinced that nursing is the linchpin in the delivery of health care in this country," Scott says. "Nurses have always brought care to people where they live."

"It is a great honor," she says, "to be able to testify in favor of your profession."

Louise Shoemaker

Born: 1925

There was never any ivory tower in Louise Shoemaker's vision of the School of Social Work at the University of Pennsylvania — or anywhere else on campus, either.

As Social Work dean, Shoemaker pushed for the establishment of the Penn Children's Center and the Faculty Staff Assistance Program, which provides free counseling and referral to health and welfare resources to all University employees.

At her instigation, the School of Social Work reached out beyond the campus to assist groups such as the Hispanic Child Welfare Training Program, the Summer Youth Project, the Philadelphia Water Department's Employee Assistance Program, and the Citizens' Committee for Children and Youth.

Under her direction, the school revised its curriculum in the 1970s to include professional education on the issue of racism for all of its graduate students and established a faculty-led racism workshop for supervisors of community agencies using the University's students.

And throughout her 14-year tenure as dean, Shoemaker worked diligently to attract more African-American students and faculty to the School of Social Work — with the result that by the time of her retirement as dean (though not as professor) in 1985, the school boasted the University's highest percentage of African-American faculty members.

For Shoemaker, it was all simply a matter of pursuing social justice, a goal she considers "at the heart" of her profession. It's a goal she has for the heart of the University, as well.

"I'd like to see the University become a more humane place for people to study and work," Shoemaker told the *Daily Pennsylvanian* in 1990.

Shoemaker credits her parents and her church upbringing for her strong sense of social activism. She was born in Clinton, Iowa, to Otto and Caroline Proehl. Her father served as a Lutheran pastor in Galveston, Texas, and as president of Wartburg College, a Lutheran college in Clinton. Shoemaker's mother was a teacher and a bank teller.

"In Texas, some parishioners didn't approve of my father's views against racism," Shoemaker recalled in an interview with a Lutheran magazine. "My parents' views have made a big difference in my life."

Shoemaker received her undergraduate degree from the University of Illinois in 1945 and at the age of 19 came east to Penn to study for her master's of social work. She received that degree two years later and immediately went into practice, spending most of the next 20 years as a social worker. She worked in settlement houses in Minneapolis, New York, and Bremen, Germany, and served as director of a home for emotionally disturbed children in St. Paul, Minn. She also served as head of staff of the training division of the Baltimore Department of Public Welfare.

Returning to Penn, she earned her doctor of social work degree in 1965. In 1971 she was named acting dean of the School of Social Work, then served as dean from 1973 to 1985. She continued as a professor at the school until 1999 and remained active in University affairs, serving as chairperson of Penn's Faculty Senate Executive Committee, as chairperson of the Association of Women Faculty and Administrators at the University, and as the first woman president of Penn's chapter of the American Association of University Professors.

The same year that she retired as dean at Penn, Shoemaker took on a multi-year commitment to develop Nigeria's first master's degree program in social work at the University of Ibadan. In six months, Shoemaker had readied the plan for a program of study. She also conducted seminars in the departments of psychiatry, preventive and social medicine, nursing, and physical therapy, and lectured in the department of sociology. She has returned to Ibadan many times since then, often leading groups of Penn students in summer study programs. The cross-cultural exchange, Shoemaker told a reporter shortly after her first trip to Nigeria, enriches both ways. Hers was an experience, she said, "that I am finding woven into what I now teach in the United States."

A lifelong member of the Evangelical Lutheran Church in America, Shoemaker has worked to highlight social justice issues there as well. She chaired a committee examining equality of women in the church and was instrumental in drafting goals for minority ministry. In 1994, Shoemaker was granted the Wittenberg Award by the Luther Institute for her many achievements as a Lutheran activist.

Just in the past year, Shoemaker has again extended herself, adopting two orphans from the Sudan who had previously spent 13 years in refugee camps. Both are now in 12th grade, and Shoemaker has high hopes that they will ultimately be able to attend college. "I'm 76," Shoemaker says. "This proves that at any age you can be helpful to others — and have a good time doing it."

At the 1991 Penn commencement, speaking as chair of the Faculty Senate, Shoemaker offered one final exhortation to graduates as they prepared to leave a University that has been transformed by her efforts. "Your education makes each one of you a member of the privileged few in the world. Use that privilege not just to make a living, but to make a difference," Shoemaker said. "As Mother Jones said in an equally turbulent and unjust era, 'Let's say a prayer for the dead and work like hell for the living.'"

Helen Dickens

I t never seems to have occurred to Helen Octavia Dickens that she couldn't be anything but what she wanted to be.

The daughter of a slave (who changed his name in homage to his favorite novelist), Dickens grew up to become a board-certified obstetrician gynecologist and professor of obstetrics and gynecology and associate dean for minority affairs at the University of Pennsylvania's School of Medicine. She was one of the first African-American women to graduate from medical school in this country and the first African-American woman to serve as a faculty member in Penn's medical school.

Dickens credits her father, who wanted her to be a nurse, for encouraging her educational aspirations. "I thought that was fine," Dickens recalled in an interview taken as part of the Black Women Physicians Project at the Medical College of Pennsylvania. "But somewhere along the way, I decided that if I was going to be a nurse, I might as well become a doctor."

Getting to her goals took self-confidence, intelligence, and the willingness to do a lot of hard work — traits that Dickens had in abundance.

Born in 1909 in Dayton, Ohio, to Charles and Darsy Dickens, Dickens was only eight years old when her father died. She moved to Chicago when she was 17 to attend Crane Junior College where tuition was free to city residents. After three years, she transferred to the medical school at the University of Illinois, the only African-American woman in her class.

Born: 1909

44

While developing her mind, Dickens was forced to toughen her outlook.

"I sat in the front seat. If other students wanted a good seat, they had to sit beside me. If they didn't, it was not my concern because I could clearly see the professor and the blackboard as I was right up there," Dickens explained. "This way I didn't have to look at them or the gestures made that were directed against me or toward me."

Graduating with her medical degree from Illinois in 1934, Dickens interned at Provident Hospital in Chicago. There she read about the family practice of pioneering African-American doctor Virginia Alexander (a sister-in-law of Sadie Alexander who recieved her undergraduate degree from Penn). Dickens moved to Philadelphia to join Alexander and worked with her for the next six years, providing both general and obstetric care to a clientele that was 95 percent African-American. It was obstetrics that captured her heart. "The first baby I saw delivered, I think that clinched it," Dickens recalled later. "Oh, a miracle!"

Hoping to specialize in the field, Dickens went back to school, enrolling at Penn for her master's degree in medical science. She returned to Provident Hospital for her residency in obstetrics and gynecology in 1942 but didn't stay long, moving on to a residency in obstetrics at Harlem Hospital in New York. In 1945, Dickens recieved her Master's of Medical Science in obstetrics and gynecology fron Penn, the first African-American to earn that degree. One year later, she was certified by the American Board of Obstetrics and Gynecology. She met and married surgeon Purvis Sinclair Henderson while in Chicago, but the couple was unable to live together for several years as they pursued residencies in different parts of the country.

After training at Harlem, Dickens returned to Philadelphia in 1948 to join the staff at Mercy Douglass Hospital.

In 1950, she became the first African-American woman to be admitted into the American College of Surgeons. Dickens served as the director of obstetrics and gynecology at Mercy Douglass until it closed in 1967. She also joined the staff at the old Women's Hospital, and in 1965, Dickens became an instructor in the department of obstetrics and gynecology at Penn. By 1966 she was an associate, rising to assistant professor in 1967, associate professor in 1970, and full professor in 1976. Dickens, who eventually served as department head, remained at Penn until her retirement in 1994.

The recipient of numerous honorary degrees, including one from Penn, Dickens was also the first recipient in 1991 of a lifetime achievement award named for her. In 1998, Penn designated its clinics on the second floor of Gates Pavilion as the Helen O. Dickens Center for Women's Health. And the College of Physicians of Philadelphia annually holds the Helen O. Dickens, M.D. Dinner to bring together minority students, alumni, faculty, and house staff.

Under Dickens' tenure, Penn pioneered model programs in teen pregnancy prevention and medical minority affairs. And she was an untiring mentor and outspoken champion for minority students who chose to attend Penn's medical school.

In a 1990 interview, Vanessa Gamble, an African-American doctor who entered Penn medical school in 1974, recalled, "I remember going in to see her once where there were some folks who made us feel as though we maybe did not belong at Penn, that we were the special admits, and that somehow we weren't up to par. Dr. Dickens said to me, 'The way I see it is that, from where we started from and where we are now, we had to be better than a lot of them to get there.'" Added Gamble, "I'll never forget her saying that."

Rebecca Brownlee

Born: 1911 Died: 1954

Rebecca Jean Brownlee wanted to teach on the college level. But even though she had earned an undergraduate degree in education and a master's and doctorate in political science and was well respected in her field, she still had one significant disadvantage when she started looking for a job in the 1940s — her sex.

"My mother taught me regularly that your worst defeats have within them the elements — if you use them — of your greatest victories," Brownlee said in a 1977 interview. "Who knows? I might have been a mediocre teacher."

Well, in fact, she wasn't, as anyone who enrolled in the courses she taught as assistant professor of political science at the University of Pennsylvania could testify. But she was a brilliant administrator, shepherding the College for Women as its third and last dean for 15 years until it became a part of the coeducational Faculty of Arts and Sciences in 1975.

"From the beginning it was an administrative unit without its own faculty or its own funds," Brownlee said of the College for Women. "Its only power was persuasion."

Persuasion, perhaps, but also example. Under Brownlee's leadership, the College for Women innovated thematic studies, the crossover between disciplines, combined degrees, and submatriculations within the University. Its individualized student advising was reportedly the open envy of the men's college, and when the two merged, Dean Vartan Gregorian tapped Brownlee for the new post of dean of advising for all undergraduates in the arts and sciences.

Brownlee was born in Philadelphia in 1911 to Robert and Margaret Stewart Brownlee. Growing up on Rittenhouse Square just across the river from the Penn campus, she attended Friends Select School, graduating in 1929. Brownlee received her certificate in elementary education from the Philadelphia Normal School in 1933 and, as Phi Beta Kappa, her bachelor's degree in education in 1934 from Penn's newly formed College for Women.

While completing her master's degree in political science, Brownlee served as directress of Sergeant Hall, Penn's new undergraduate women's residence on 34th Street. ("The first winter I was there, we had five appendectomies," Brownlee recalled in 1977. "Now you don't have five appendectomies in 144 students, but we had them. I maintain that appendectomies are endemic.")

Earning her doctorate in 1942, Brownlee spent the war years as the chief local administrator with the Civil Service Commission — then the highest post held by a woman in Philadelphia.

In the absence of offers for a full-time teaching position, Brownlee returned to Penn in 1946 as personnel officer for the College for Women, although she quickly wrangled an appointment to teach part time in the political science department as well. In 1958 she was named acting dean and in 1959 became dean of the College for Women.

Although she ostensibly retired in 1977, Brownlee never severed her relationship with the University. Named dean emeritus in 1981, Brownlee turned her considerable organizational abilities towards reviving the Friends of the Library of the University of Pennsylvania, serving as chairman of the group from 1982 to 1985. From 1989 until her death she was an overseer of the library.

Among her many awards were Penn's 1963 Alumna Award of Merit and an honorary doctorate of laws from Penn in 1986.

Of all her achievements, however, Brownlee claimed the greatest pride in a vicarious one: the many accomplishments of alumnae of the College for Women. "You think, perhaps, that you contributed a little bit to it," she said in 1977. "There are an awful lot of alums out there doing swell things." Brownlee was also touched, she said, when a former student dedicated his book on ballistic missiles to the teacher who had started him on his career in political science. "That's," she said, "psychic income of the highest order."

Virginia Knauer

Born: 1915

Before Virginia Knauer established the Consumer Information Center within the federal General Services Administration in 1970, Pueblo, Colo., had no resonance in the public mind. Now Pueblo's 81009 Zip Code is instantly recognizable as the source of an enormous trove of information and guidance on everything from hormone replacement therapy to buying homes with low down payments. It was one of the many initiatives Knauer championed during her years as special assistant for consumer affairs to Presidents Nixon, Ford, and Reagan that effectively re-oriented the nation's outlook on consumer issues.

Knauer was born in Philadelphia in 1915 to Herman and Helen Harrington Wright. Highly artistic, she attended Girls' High and enrolled in Penn's School of Fine Arts but also attended the Pennsylvania Academy of Fine Arts on a Mayor's scholarship. Graduating from Penn in 1937 with a bachelor's degree in fine arts, Knauer went abroad for post-graduate study at the Royal Academy of Fine Arts in Florence, Italy.

In 1940, she married Philadelphia attorney Wilhelm Knauer and devoted herself to raising their two children. But she kept active in civic and political groups, founding the Greater Northeast Philadelphia Republican Women's Club in 1956 and serving as a delegate or an alternate to the 1960, 1964, and 1968 Republican national conventions.

Knauer's conversion to the cause of consumer protection came after she was elected to Philadelphia's City Council in 1959. "Everything we ran into was some sort of consumer problem," Knauer recalled in a 1994 interview. "Things people call on their council member to provide."

After serving two terms on the council, Knauer took her experience statewide, becoming head of the Pennsylvania Bureau of Consumer Protection in 1968. It was in Pennsylvania that Knauer started producing consumer brochures, and the results were dramatic. In her first year of office, the number of complaints processed by her bureau rose from 2,803 to 4,888.

In 1969, President Nixon tapped Knauer to serve as his full-time special assistant for consumer affairs. In that position, which she held until 1977, she was also the U.S. representative and vice chairman of the Committee on Consumer Policy of the Organization for Economic Cooperation and Development, which meets twice yearly in Paris.

In addition to establishing the consumer information clearinghouse in Pueblo, Knauer designed and began publishing Consumer News, a newsletter that compiled information on consumer programs and activities in all federal agencies. She represented the consumer's point of view on a number of cabinet-level committees, including the Council on Wage and Price Stability and the Cost of Living Council. And she served as a mentor to many of the young women flocking to Washington in the 1970s and 1980s to pursue careers in government. (Knauer secured her Harvard-trained assistant Elizabeth Hanford a seat on the Federal Trade Commission and also introduced her to her future husband, U.S. Senator Bob Dole.)

In 1981, President Reagan appointed Knauer his special advisor for consumer affairs and director of the U.S. Office of Consumer Affairs, a position she held until 1988. It was during this time that Knauer began distributing the Consumer's Resource Handbook, a complaint manual for consumers that has become one of the government's most popular publications.

Knauer is the recipient of many honorary degrees, including an honorory doctor of laws from Penn in 1971. In 1977, she won the Philadelphia Award and in 1984 was honored with Penn's Founders Day Award for Public Service.

In retirement she has returned to her artistic roots, painting portraits and lecturing on historic preservation, antique furniture, and 18th-century ceramics, areas of lifelong interest. One of Knauer's early restoration efforts, the pre-Revolutionary Man Full of Trouble Tavern in Philadelphia's Society Hill neighborhood, which she renovated and equipped as a museum of Colonial decorative arts a number of years ago, was recently donated to Penn by the Knauer Foundation for Historic Preservation (founded by Knauer and her late husband), for use as a faculty residence.

Having devoted most of her professional career to improving the flow of information about products and services in this country, Knauer can take pride in the resurgence of what she has called the basic principle guiding the nation's business: "Satisfaction guaranteed, or your money back."

Denise Scott Brown

Born: 1931

*M*iami's art deco South Beach, Galveston, Texas' historic commercial district, and the charming Victorian Main Street of Jim Thorpe, Pa., are all lively neighborhoods. Property values are stable and civic pride is high.

But that was not the case more than 30 years ago when young architect and urban planner Denise Scott Brown rescued them from the wrecking ball of urban renewal.

For University of Pennsylvania alumni, an even more startling example of Scott Brown's vision sits on the edge of College Hall green. As one of Penn's junior faculty members in 1960, Brown attended a University meeting where plans to tear down the Frank Furness Library were being discussed. Knowing she held a minority opinion but steeled by the courage of her convictions, Scott Brown stood up and gave an impassioned plea to spare the building. The reaction was stony. But after the meeting, Scott Brown was approached by another young instructor named Robert Venturi who told her, "You know, I agreed with every word you said."

"Well, then," Scott Brown reportedly demanded, "why didn't you speak up?"

Some 25 years later, Venturi and Scott Brown, by then married and co-partners in the architectural firm of Venturi, Scott Brown and Associates, were awarded the contract to renovate the Furness Building, now considered one of the architectural jewels of the Penn campus.

Scott Brown, who was born in 1931 in rural Zambia and raised in Johannesburg, South Africa, came by her architectural sensibility naturally. Her father, Shim Lakofski, ran a prosperous real estate development firm, and her mother, Phyllis, had studied architecture before her marriage.

"At about five I knew I was going to be an architect because my mother had studied architecture," Scott Brown recalls. "I thought it was women's

50

work. I had a proprietary feeling about architecture. I could own it because my mother owned it."

In 1948 she enrolled at the University of Witwatersrand, but in the fourth year of a five-year architectural program, Scott Brown decided to pursue an apprenticeship in an architect's office in London. While there, she enrolled at the Architectural Association School of Architecture and received her degree in 1955.

That same year, she married fellow South African architecture student Robert Scott Brown. The two moved to Philadelphia in 1958 with the intention of studying under architect Louis I. Kahn but mistakenly enrolled in Penn's city planning school. It was an inspired mistake.

Sizing up what was then a fierce debate between city planners and architects, Scott Brown found she could straddle both camps. She earned her master's degree in city planning from Penn in 1960 despite the tragic death of her husband in an auto accident the year before. She stayed on as an instructor, teaching budding architects about urban design and urban design students about architecture and earned a master's in architecture from Penn in 1965.

After their exchange about the Furness Building, Venturi and Scott Brown became friends. But it wasn't until Scott Brown left Penn for the West Coast in 1965, first as a visiting professor at Berkeley and then to help start the architecture school at UCLA, that the relationship became serious, cemented perhaps by their mutual fascination with the strip development of the American West, particularly Las Vegas.

In 1967 the two married and Scott Brown moved back East. Teaching together at Yale University, Venturi and Scott Brown cultivated the theories that later found fruit in their 1972 controversial book, *Learning from Las Vegas*. A treatise on the symbolism of architectural form, the book suggests that supermarket parking lots or gambling casino signs can provide valuable lessons in

design. It was, Scott Brown writes, "a plea to architects to broaden their sights."

Unafraid to confront the architectural establishment, Venturi and Scott Brown only slowly gained the respect of their profession. Through the 1970s and 1980s, their firm pioneered preservation projects around the country. They also worked for a number of universities — including Penn — to revamp and improve their campus plans.

Recent years have brought escalating acclaim to both the firm and its principals. Critics around the world hailed Venturi and Scott Brown's design for the Sainsbury Wing at the National Gallery in London, which opened in 1991. In May 2001 the French government conferred medals of the Order of Arts and Letters on the pair for the design of an 866,000-square-foot government administrative complex in Toulouse, France. Scott Brown also has been honored with the National Medal of Arts, the U.S. Presidential Award, the Chicago Architecture Award, and the Italian Commendatore of the Order of Merit. The Association of Collegiate Schools of Architecture has named her a distinguished professor.

Although she participates in all aspects of the business of Venturi, Scott Brown and Associates, Scott Brown is perhaps best known for her urban planning and design. Describing her philosophy in 1981, Scott Brown wrote, "In small towns or urban neighborhoods, social, economic, and physical problems often occur against a backdrop of once splendid or admirable architecture. We try to plan in a nurturing way to help existing occupants make economic reuse of this architectural heritage that surrounds them."

"As a planner," she continued, "the vision of the world I'd like to be part of creating is pragmatic, not utopian. By understanding the forces that are shaping, or misshaping, the town or city, I hope to help its citizens use these forces to get where they want to go."

Judith Rodin

In an address to undergraduates attending Penn's 1998 Women in Leadership Series, Judith Rodin spoke about a new breed of leaders: "They are decisive enablers, people who recognize that good leadership is helping one's students, colleagues, and employees to be better at what they do. It is governing with soul."

Rodin, who is Penn's seventh president and the first woman president in the Ivy League, could have been describing herself. Since beginning her presidency in 1994, Rodin has enabled the University to grow in sometimes startling new directions. And she's put her soul into it.

One of her first actions as Penn's new president was the groundbreaking resolution of a Title IX dispute, assuring that the University's female athletes received the same level of support as their male counterparts.

In the belief that it was ineffective anyway and that it sent a message of ideological conformity that stifled creative discourse, she abolished the University's speech code, which criminalized the use of racial, ethnic, or sexual slurs.

Under Rodin's direction, Penn now offers more than 60 service-learning courses for students seeking to assist in enduring community improvements in the University's West Philadelphia neighborhood. At the same time, Penn, the Philadelphia School District, and the teachers' union have formed a partnership to build a neighborhood elementary school.

Born: 1944

One of Penn's strategic goals developed during Rodin's tenure is the globalization of Penn's outreach, both in research and scholarly collaboration, but also in attracting and recruiting international students who are likely to assume leadership roles when they return to their home countries.

Looking to the future, Rodin has actively encouraged the mission of the Trustees Council of Penn Women, a group of high-achieving women leaders who in ten years have raised more than $13 million to support programs that strengthen the position of women in education, particularly at Penn.

"Personally, I have had the great fortune of doing rich and rewarding work since my days as a Penn undergraduate," Rodin said in 1998. Great fortune, yes, but great fortune assisted by a lot of hard work.

Born in Philadelphia to Morris Seitz, supervisor of auditors for the sales tax division of the Common-wealth of Pennsylvania, and Sally Winson Seitz, Rodin attended Girls' High, graduating in 1962. She came to Penn thinking of majoring in French, but an introductory psychology course changed her mind. While creating an academic niche for herself, Rodin was also active in student politics, serving as president of the Women's Student Government Association. Working with her male counterpart, Rodin bucked tradition to merge the women's and men's government groups into one organization.

"Short term, there were many who were resistant to this change," Rodin recalled. "Long term, there's no question that this is what was needed to strengthen Penn's student body. We didn't do it to win popularity votes; we did it because we were willing to take a stand."

Graduating Phi Beta Kappa in 1966, Rodin went on to Columbia University, where she earned a doctorate in psychology in 1970. Following a National Science Foundation post-doctoral fellowship at the University of California at Irvine, Rodin became assistant professor of psychology at Yale, rising to become the first female chair of the department of psychology, dean of the Yale Graduate School of Arts and Sciences, and, eventually, University Provost. When she was tapped to become Penn's seventh president in 1994, she became Penn's first alumna to serve her alma mater as president.

"Leadership is not for the faint of heart," Rodin cautioned in her 1998 address to undergraduates. "You are going to need many of the skills necessary for a successful entrepreneur — commitment, vision, and energy; a talent for communicating; the willingness to take risks, to be accountable, and to take responsibility. And most of all, the faith to believe in one self and one's dreams despite what others may say."

It's a tall order, but it can be done.

"None of us," Rodin said, speaking of herself in words that could be applied to all of Franklin's daughters, "started as confident as we may look today."

The Heritage Continues

In the Arts...

In Service...

In Sports...

In Community...

In Action...

EDUCATION
BEWA

Photo and Research Resources

The order of resources listed follows the order of profiles in the book.

PAGE 6

Easby, Flanigen, Gannett

Photo of three chemists, Collections of the University of Pennsylvania Archives and Records Center; Photo of Gannett, courtesy of the Rochester Museum and Science Center, Rochester, N.Y.; Photo of Easby, Collections of the University of Pennsylvania Archives and Records.

Gertrude Klein Peirce Easby: Archives, University of Pennsylvania; Bohning, James J. "Women in Chemistry at Penn 1894-1908: Edgar Fahs Smith as Mentor" in Chemical Heritage (Newsmagazine of the Chemical Heritage Foundation), Volume 19, Number 1, Spring 2001

Anna Flanigen: Archives, University of Pennsylvania; Bohning, ibid.; Archives, Mount Holyoke College.

Mary Thorn Lewis Gannett: Archives, University of Pennsylvania; Archives, University of Rochester: Bohning, ibid.; Library, Rochester Museum & Science Center; Western New York Suffragists website http://winningthevote.org/MLGannett.html; Rochester Democrat and Chronicle, October 25,1952.

PAGE 10

Alice Bennett

Photo of Bennett, courtesy of the Medical College of Pennsylvania - Hahnemann University Archives and Special Collections.

Archives, University of Pennsylvania; American National Biography (ANB) published under the auspices of the American Council of Learned Societies, John A. Garraty and Mark C. Carnes, General Editors. Oxford University Press, N.Y. 1999; Archives and Special Collections, Women's Medical College of Pennsylvania - Hahnemann University (Drexel University); Archives, Norristown State Hospital; McCormick-International Harvester Collection Archives, State Historical Society of Wisconsin; McGovern, Constance M. "Doctors or Ladies? Women Physicians in Psychiatric Institutions, 1872-1900," Bulletin of the History of Medicine, Vol. 55, pp. 88-107.

PAGE 12

Carrie Kilgore

Photo of Kilgore, Collections of the University of Pennsylvania Archives and Records Center.

ANB; Archives, University of Pennsylvania; Maurer, Elizabeth K., "The Sphere of Carrie Burnham Kilgore," Temple Law Review 65 (3), 1992.

PAGE 14

Emily Gregory

Photo of Gregory, courtesy of the Barnard College Library.

Archives, University of Pennsylvania; ANB; Barnard College Library; Britton, Elizabeth G., Bulletin of the Torrey Botanical Club, May 29, 1897; Schmid, Rudolf, "Botanical text books," an unpublished manuscript (1897) by Emily Lovira Gregory (1841-1897) on plant anatomy textbooks
Bulletin of the Torrey Botanical Club, 1987, pp. 307-324.

PAGE 16

Ida Asbury

Photo of young Asbury, courtesy of the Moorland-Spingarn Research Center, Howard University; photo of older Asbury, Collections of the University of Pennsylvania Archives and Records Center.

Archives, University of Pennsylvania; Moorland-Spingarn Research Center, Howard University.

PAGE 18

Anna Lindsay

Photo of Lindsay, courtesy of Wellesley College Archives.

Archives, University of Pennsylvania; Wellesley College Archives.

PAGE 20

Mary Pennington

Photo of Pennington, Collections of the University of Pennsylvania Archives and Records Center.

Archives, University of Pennsylvania; Bohning, ibid.; ANB; Heggie, Barbara, "The Ice Woman," The New Yorker, September 6, 1941.

PAGE 22

Margaret Klingelsmith

Photo of Klingelsmith, Collections of the University of Pennsylvania Archives and Records Center.

Archives, University of Pennsylvania; Katzenstein, Caroline, Lifting the Curtain: The State and National Woman Suffrage Campaigns in Pennsylvania as I Saw Them Dorrance & Co., Inc, Philadelphia, 1955.

PAGE 24

Alice Paul

Photo of Paul in academic robes, courtesy of the National Museum of American History, Smithsonian Institution, and the Alice Paul Centennial Foundation; photo of Paul celebrating passage of the 19th Amendment, courtesy of the Library of Congress Prints and Photographs Division.

ANB; Archives, University of Pennsylvania; Irwin, Inez Haynes, Alice Paul and the National Women's Party, Denlinger's Publishers, Ltd. Fairfax, Va., 1964; Di Martino, Joan M. The Lost Mosaic Piece: The development of Alice Paul's Militancy in Philadelphia Suffrage, 1910-1912. Rutgers University, unpublished M.A. thesis, 1998; Archives, The Alice Paul Centennial Foundation; Alice Paul Collection, the Schlesinger Library, Radcliffe Institute, Harvard University; Suffragists website http://sunsite.berkeley.edu:2020/teiproj/oh/suffragists.

PAGE 28

Sadie Alexander

Photo of Alexander in academic robes, Collections of the University of Pennsylvania Archives and Records Center; photo of older Alexander by G.M. Wilson, Collections of the University of Pennsylvania Archives and Records Center.

Alexander Family Papers, Archives, University of Pennsylvania; ANB; Epperson, Lia B., Knocking Down Doors: The Trailblazing Life of Sadie Tanner Mossell Alexander (Stanford University Law School, Women's Legal History Project, 1998, available on the Internet in PDF format).

PAGE 32

Gladys Tantaquidgeon

Photo of Tantaquidgeon, courtesy of the Mohegan Tribe.

Archives, University of Pennsylvania; Archives, University of Pennsylvania Museum; Martin, Douglas, "The Medicine Woman of the Mohegans," The New York Times, June 4, 1997; Tantaquidgeon, Gladys, Folk Medicine of the Delaware and Related Algonkian Indians, Harrisburg, Pennsylvania Historical Commission Anthropological Papers #3, 1972; Tantaquidgeon, Gladys

and Fawcett, Jayne G, "Symbolic Motifs
on Painted Baskets of the Mohegan-
Pequot" in A Key into the Language
of Woodsplint Baskets, Edited by Ann
McMullen and Russell G. Handsmar,
American Indian Archeological Institute,
Washington, Conn., 1987; Fawcett,
Melissa Jayne, Medicine Trail: The Life
and Lessons of Gladys Tantaquidgeon,
Tucson, University of Arizona Press,
2000; Fawcett, Melissa Jayne, "The Role
of Gladys Tantaquidgeon," Papers of the
Fifteenth Algonquian Conference, Edited
by William Cowan, Ottawa 1984; Nichols,
Peter, "Running Against Time; Medicine
Woman Preserves Mohegan Culture,"
PENN Arts & Sciences, Summer, 2001;
Pat Grandjean, "The Elder," Connecticut,
August 1992.

PAGE 34

Sister Constance Murphy

Photo of Murphy, courtesy of Sisterhood
of Saint John the Divine.

Archives, University of Pennsylvania;
Personal interview, July 4, 2001; Anglican
Diocese of Toronto; Other Little Ships:
Memoirs of Sister Constance, SSJD,
The Patmos Press, Toronto, 1997; The
Sisterhood of St. John the Divine website,
http://www.ssjd.ca/index.html.

PAGE 36

Ruth Klein

Photo of Klein, Collections of the
University of Pennsylvania Archives
and Records Center.

Archives, University of Pennsylvania;
Archives, Oak Lane Presbyterian Church;
The Philadelphia High School for Girls
Alumnae News, Winter 1999.

PAGE 38

Althea Hottel

Photo of Hottel, Collections of the
University of Pennsylvania Archives
and Records Center.

Archives, University of Pennsylvania,
Oral History; Delta Delta Delta archives,
The Trident, May 1928 and March 1929.

PAGE 40

Jesse Scott

Photo of Scott, courtesy of Joan Lynaugh.

Personal interview, June 29, 2001; University of Pennsylvania School of Nursing; "History of School of Nursing" http://www/nursing.upenn.edu/news/history.htm.

PAGE 42

Louise Shoemaker

Photo of Shoemaker by Frank Ross, Collections of the University of Pennsylvania Archives and Records Center.

Personal papers; Personal interview, Sept. 5, 2001; "A Voice for the have-nots," The Lutheran, June 15, 1983; "Social Workers Celebrate the Human Family," The Pennsylvania Gazette, May 1985; "Humanizing a School: A Case Study," Entrée, Dec., 1988; "SEC Chair-elect Shoemaker highly regarded among peers," The Daily Pennsylvanian, April 17, 1990; "Dr. Louise P. Shoemaker: Citizen of the World," Sociolog, Fall 1991; "New Programs Praised by Participants," The Rotarian, May 1992.

PAGE 44

Helen Dickens

Photo of Dickens, Collections of the University of Pennsylvania Archives and Records Center.

Archives, University of Pennsylvania Medical School; Penn Medicine - Penn Medical Center, Fall 1990, Volume IV "Just Do It." Edited by Dennis A. Dinan; "Helen Octavia Dickens" by Elizabeth Astras, website of Albion College, Mi. http://educte.albion.edu/art/aframsci/elizabeth.htm.

PAGE 46

Rebecca Brownlee

Photo of Brownlee, courtesy of the Office of Development, University Libraries of the University of Pennsylvania.

Archives, University of Pennsylvania; "The dean," The Pennsylvania Gazette, May 1977; Friends of the Penn Library http://www.library.upenn.edu/friends/brownlee.html.

PAGE 48

Virginia Knauer

Photo of Knauer by Norman J. Tavan, courtesy of the U.S. Department of Health and Human Services.

Personal Papers; "Her forte was consumer rights," St. Petersburg Times, Jan. 23, 1994; website of the Salisbury, N.C. Post http://www.salisburypost.com/liddy/liddydole031999.htm.; A Few Good Women website http://afgw.libraries.psu.edu; Distinguished Women website of Northwood University http://www.northwood.edu/dw/1997/knauer.html.

PAGE 50

Denise Scott Brown

Photo of Scott Brown by Julie Marquart for Venturi, Scott Brown and Associates.

Architectural Archives, University of Pennsylvania; Gabor, Andrea, Einstein's Wife: Work and Marriage in the Lives of Five Great American Women, (August 1996) "Denise Scott Brown;" Venturi, Scott Brown & Associates, Philadelphia, Pa..

PAGE 52

Judith Rodin

Photo of Rodin, courtesy of the Office of Development and Alumni Relations, University of Pennsylvania; photo of young Rodin from the 1966 Record, Collections of the University of Pennsylvania Archives and Records Center.

Office of the President. University of Pennsylvania.

About the Authors

Linda Mallon has worked as a journalist since her graduation from the University of Pennsylvania in 1975. In addition to reporting and editing at newspapers in New York and New Jersey, she covered legislative and public policy issues as a reporter for the Washington Bureau of *Modern Maturity*. As a freelance book critic she has had numerous book reviews published in *USA Today*. She is currently assistant managing editor for newsletters for the American Academy of Actuaries in Washington, D.C. A Washington resident, she is married to economist John Mueller. They are the parents of Christian, Peter, and Lucy.

Anita Sama graduated from the University of Pennsylvania in 1973, was a Thouron Scholar at the University of St. Andrews where she earned an M.Litt. in history, and received an M.S. from Columbia's Graduate School of Journalism in 1976. She has been with the Gannett Company for 25 years, first in New York and then Washington, D.C, joining the *USA Today* staff in 1989. During that time she held a variety of editing roles in news and features and now is planning and administrative editor for the newspaper's Life section. She lives in Chevy Chase, Md. with architect husband Christopher Ruffing. They are the parents of Emily and Hilary.